YOUR KNOWLEDGE HAS VALUE

- We will publish your bachelor's and master's thesis, essays and papers

- Your own eBook and book - sold worldwide in all relevant shops

- Earn money with each sale

Upload your text at www.GRIN.com and publish for free

The Representation of Time in Fitzgerald's "Benjamin Button"

Bibliographic information published by the German National Library:

The German National Library lists this publication in the National Bibliography; detailed bibliographic data are available on the Internet at http://dnb.dnb.de.

> ISBN: 9783389090213
> This book is also available as an ebook.

© GRIN Publishing GmbH
Trappentreustraße 1
80339 München

All rights reserved

Print and binding: Books on Demand GmbH, Norderstedt, Germany
Printed on acid-free paper from responsible sources.

The present work has been carefully prepared. Nevertheless, authors and publishers do not incur liability for the correctness of information, notes, links and advice as well as any printing errors.

GRIN web shop: https://www.grin.com/document/1518136

The Representation of Time
in Fitzgerald's *Benjamin Button*

Using Time to Challenge Prevailing Age Roles

Contents

1 Introduction and Preliminary Remarks 3

2 General Representation of Time in American Literature up to the Modernist Era 4

3 The Emergence of Age as a Social Category 5

    3.1 The 'Normal Biography' 6

    3.2 The Fear of Old Age 7

4 Analysis of Fitzgerald's Temporal Structuring and its Underlying Motivations 8

    4.1 Benjamin Button's Three Threads of Age 8

        4.1.1 Chronological Age 9

        4.1.2 Physical Age 9

        4.1.3 Psychological Age 9

    4.2 Situating the Story in Reality 10

    4.3 Changes in the Protagonist's Relationships 11

    4.4 Challenging the Concept of Age 12

5 Conclusion and Final Remarks 14

6 References 15

Introduction and Preliminary Remarks

In our modern times, there is a shift away from a fixed biography. In recent decades, the trend has been against a strictly set life course. Instead, people tend to shape the stages of their lives more individually: teenagers have children or start their own businesses, retirees get married or go to university again. It shows a departure from societal expectations and age roles, such as were still common in the mid-20th century, and demonstrates a new freedom in shaping one's own identity. Even though even today life courses that deviate from the norm are sometimes viewed critically by society, an individual is seldom truly restricted by this in his freedom to take decisive steps as he chooses.

Social age roles are also addressed by Francis Scott Fitzgerald in his short story *The Curious Case of Benjamin Button* from 1922. The story follows the life of the main character Benjamin Button, who is born a 70-year-old old man and grows younger every year until he reaches babyhood and finally dies. As his environment progresses normally, he keeps coming into conflict with society because of his appearance and abilities that do not match his age. Nevertheless, the protagonist manages to be quite successful: he goes to university, becomes a war veteran, runs his own business, gets married and has a child, though not in the usual order.

The following paper will show that Fitzgerald uses Benjamin Button's special condition and the associated depiction of time in the short story to challenge the age roles that were prevalent in society at the time of publication. For this purpose, the general representation of time up to the Jazz Age, which Fitzgerald can be assigned to, will be illustrated first. Then, the age roles prevalent in the Jazz Age of the early 20th century will be examined more closely. Among other things, the concept of the 'Normal Biography' coined by Michael Basseler as well as the fear of old age and the rejuvenation projects made possible by new scientific methods will be discussed. Furthermore, an analysis of Fitzgerald's temporal structuring is carried out in order to understand the background and motivations of the same. For this purpose, the short story is examined on the basis of the three threads of age: Benjamin Button's chronological age, physical age, and psychological age. Then, the importance of situating the story in reality is analyzed and the changes in Benjamin Button's relationships will be discussed. Finally, the criticism of the concept of age through the protagonist's reverse biography is highlighted before a final conclusion closes the paper.

General Representation of Time in American Literature up to the Modernist Era

> [N]arrativity and temporality are closely related. Indeed, I take temporality to be that structure that reaches language in narrativity and narrativity to be the language structure that has temporality as its ultimate referent. Their relationship is therefore reciprocal. (Ricoeur 169)

Ricoeur's statement illustrates the special significance that time has and always had in narratives. Nevertheless, the representation of time has changed constantly throughout literary history. Similarly, Miller asserts that "[e]ach literary work has a different time sense - even those by the same author" (87). However, tendencies toward certain representations of temporality can be discerned in certain literary periods.

The original technique of representing time consists of a straightforward chronological plot that covers a person's entire life or, in shorter narratives, only a fragment of it (What Exactly Is Time? 27). This can be considered the standard method of structuring a story in time and has been the medium of choice in English and world literature for several centuries. Nevertheless, even in early literature there were works that deviated from a purely chronological account and included, for example, flashbacks, such as Homer's Odyssey from the 8th century BC (What Exactly Is Time? 35).

It was not until the fin de siècle that time in literature received gradually more attention and "by highlighting the temporality of stories, time [became] the primary subject of those narratives" (Basseler 2). One of the most famous modern authors who experimented with the representation of time was Marcel Proust, neglecting constraints of linear time and mixing past, present, and future through flashbacks and flashforwards. In general, "the use of temporal distortion, fragmentation and non-linear timelines in novels became popular tools" (What Exactly Is Time? 42) from the 20th century onwards.

However, at first glance, *The Curious Case of Benjamin Button* follows a linear and chronological structure that encompasses the life of the main character and is not at all different from the original representation of time in earlier periods. In fact, the short story is distinguished by the fact that only individual aspects do not follow the usual course of time, but instead run backwards, namely the physical age of the protagonist. This particular constellation, which results in Benjamin Button's life running counter to that of his fellow human beings, brings time and its associated effects on the human body to the fore.

The Emergence of Age as a Social Category

Age has not always had the importance in society that it has today. Certainly, we have always recognized the age of other people, since the ever-changing age-dependent appearance is the first thing we recognize when we meet new people. Yet it wasn't until the 19th and 20th centuries that society decided to ascribe roles and expectations to a particular age. American historian Howard Chudacoff considers the reason for this to be industrialization and the changes it brought: "[S]cientific virtues - such as rationalization, precision, numerical measurement, or scheduling - were transferred to the human life course" (Wohlmann 38). Thus, time took over from space as the main factor determining our identity, while the latter was still defining our financial and social status in the centuries before (Basseler 1).

The new efficiency-driven industry replaced workers who were too old with fresh new recruits, creating distinct life stages, such as childhood, preceding the working career, and old age, succeeding the working career. As a result, age became not only a biological marker, but also a social marker that influences our behavior and our attitudes and expectations towards others. "Age is thus a lens through which we have learned to assess people. It has become a crucial social category, similar to class, race, and gender" (Wohlmann 41). Compared to race or gender, what is striking about age is that it is not constant but changes throughout life, making the process of aging even more important in today's world.

As a result of this greater significance, we also evaluate ourselves based on our age, creating what is referred to as age identity (Gullette 15). Our age identity depends on the different conceptions of age and the process of aging that we have encountered throughout our lives. Parents, mentors, and friends show us their age identities in what they do and say, thus influencing our own. Even so, the society and culture in which we live also contribute to our age identities. For example, African and European youth have a completely different assessment of what stage of life they should be in. So basically, each of us has an individual age identity, but because of the strong influence of society and the narrow environment, which in turn has been influenced by society, most people in a culture have, in a sense, a very similar idea of where they should be at their age.

The 'Normal Biography'

The division of our lives into stages, the temporalization of life, so to speak, ultimately led to a "chronologically standardized life-course model, the 'normal biography'" (Basseler 5). This clear, socially accepted plan of how a life should proceed applies equally to our work and family life.

At the time *The Curious Case of Benjamin Button* was published, a boy of high social standing, as the protagonist was, was expected to learn and prepare for his place in society during childhood. Subsequently, in addition to military service, he was expected to continue his education at a university before starting his own business or continuing the family business. At the same time, he was faced with the task of finding a wife and having children. He was to fill these roles until he retired due to old age and optimally handed over the company to his son, who in turn would follow the same life path. Any deviations from this life course were viewed critically by society and resulted in conflict, as the later analysis will show. Interestingly, a century ago, a woman's life course was still quite different from a man's, due in part to the lower political and social position of women. This discrepancy will be discussed again in more detail in 4.3.

Ultimately, this means that as we age, "we traverse age categories in the direction of the so-called arrow of time" (Medovoi 658), from which any discrepancies cause corresponding reactions. This life course is so compartmentalized against deviations within a culture that we deliberately speak only of the one life course that is so "universal in its process as the biologized body" (Gullette 15). The question arises why we as a society put so much pressure on ourselves to meet certain expectations at a certain age that we deprive ourselves of any possibility of living our lives deterministically. Industrialization has created a system that enforces these age expectations not only socially, but also politically, by issuing birth, marriage, and death certificates that carry tax implications, for example, leaving no chance for those who deviate from the norm. Freeman even goes so far as to say that, "In the eyes of the state, this sequence of socioeconomically 'productive" moments is what it means to have a life at all" (5).

The Fear of Old Age

As mentioned earlier, with the onset of industrialization, large firms characterized by anonymity began the practice of replacing workers at advanced ages with younger, more energetic ones. In this respect, the fear of old age and the process of aging itself is not surprising. However, it is not only the constant pressure of no longer finding a place at an advanced age in a working world in which protection against dismissal and similar old-age safeguards were non-existent, but also society's view of old people. They were considered useless as they were supposed to make room for the younger generations and their ideas and "expected to quiet down, keep out of the way, and contemplate the setting of the sun at the end of the day" (Port 5). As scientific possibilities increased, life expectancy continued to rise, but this also meant that older people had to be cared for correspondingly longer and more intensively, ultimately increasing the sense of burden on society.

In our Western culture, the fact that a person's physical as well as mental ability inevitably continues to decline in old age has been immediately dismissed as uselessness and weight for society to bear (Port 5). The very term *old age* shows a deviation from the social norm - one that cannot be reversed and therefore triggers such a fear of aging in people (Wohlmann 39). This perception within our society has gone so far that aging is immediately associated with declining and ultimately even dying (Port 3). Today, this assumption is still widespread, causing children to hold "some preexisting negative views about old age" (Gullette 7). This still common belief is challenged by *The Curious Case of Benjamin Button*, as Port points out that, "[f]oregrounding and defamiliarizing the effects of aging, such narratives raise significant questions about the physical and psychological manifestations of old age, as well as about characteristic narratives of progress and decline" (7).

Analysis of Fitzgerald's Temporal Structuring and its Underlying Motivations

Benjamin Button's Three Threads of Age

Three threads of age can be identified in the short story, which Henry Alexander calls chronological, physical, and psychological age (Basseler 4). In a normal person, they would run in the same direction and at the same speed. For the protagonist Benjamin Button, however, these strands do not correspond, but rather proceed completely differently.

He is born in the body of a 70-year-old old man, and as he ages, his physical appearance rejuvenates. Thus, his chronological aging and physical aging are exactly opposite to each other. For instance, on his 20th birthday he has the body of a 50-year-old and on his 65th birthday he has the body of a 5-year-old. Thus, his chronological and physical ages continue to converge before they align in his 35th year of life and then diverge again. This discrepancy between these two threads of his age offers ironic effects and provides some criticisms of the expectations of a certain age in society. The third age strand concerns Benjamin's psychological age, that is, his maturity, "which hardly seems to undergo much change, except for his final years when he gradually loses his ability to speak and finally his consciousness" (Basseler 4).

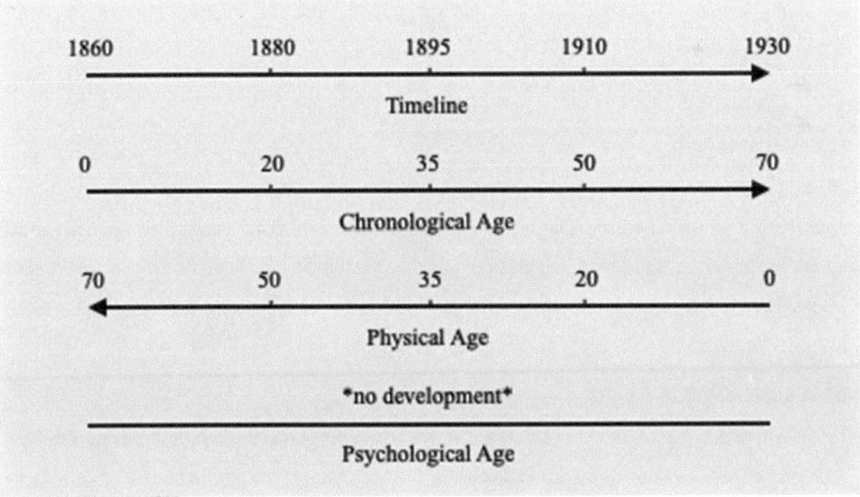

Benjamin Button's chronological age runs according to the norm. In this respect, therefore, he is no different from his fellow human beings. He is born in the hospital in 1860 and ages by one year with each passing year. Finally, he dies at home as a 70-year-old man. This chronological age is also used for government issued certificates such as his birth certificate, which combined with his physical appearance causes problems. For example, when he enrolls at Yale College, the registrar expects an 18-year-old boy. Instead, Benjamin shows up with the body of a 52-year-old. The registrar accordingly meets him with disbelief: "Now surely, Mr. Button, you don't expect me to believe that" (Fitzgerald 13).

Physical Age

Benjamin's physical aging is ultimately the crucial aspect that makes the progression of life central to the short story and deals with the question of how society expects one to look or behave according to a certain age (Port 13). Born in the body of a 70-year-old with white hair, "he 'grows' younger and younger" (Basseler 4). His hair becomes grey and later brown, as he watches his body become stronger and reach the pinnacle of his physical abilities. However, his reversed process of aging also means that he shrinks when he reaches his 50's. This is especially evident when he gradually loses his athletic ability on the football team at Yale. While he is still the best player in his first year of college, his performance in his junior year is poor, as "he had lost weight, and it seemed to the more observant among them that he was not quite as tall as before" (Fitzgerald 23). His interests are also tied to his physical age. Thus, after his birth, Benjamin finds pleasure in browsing encyclopedia and smoking cigars (Fitzgerald 10).

Psychological Age

Benjamin Button's psychological age is definitely the most difficult to identify. His mind and maturity do not seem to be developing or regressing; he seems to have the psychological age of a middle-aged man. It is only when his body reaches the toddler stage that he forgets more about his past and confines himself to the few things around him. Thus, his psychological age is more in line with his physical age, considering also how he sees his wife (Fitzgerald 22).

Situating the Story in Reality

Fitzgerald makes his critique of society's prevailing age roles and expectations during the Jazz Age particularly evident through the setting of his short story The Curious Case of Benjamin Button. By placing this fictional story about a man who ages backwards in a society that exists in reality, he is able to point out its flaws in a particularly impressive way. Numerous references to various wars, historical periods, or American society around the fin de siècle situate Benjamin Button in the real world (Basseler 3).

Benjamin Button was born in 1860 into a wealthy and socially respectable family in Baltimore. Right at the beginning, the reference to the Civil War is made by talking about an "ante-bellum Baltimore" (Fitzgerald 1) and the affiliation of the same to the "Confederacy" (Fitzgerald 1). Also, the mention of Yale College in Connecticut as a prestigious institution of higher learning ensures that it is clear to the reader at the outset that the story can be placed both spatially and temporally in America's real past. At the same time, however, he emphasizes the fictionality of the short story by naming the two fictional families *This* and *That* (Fitzgerald 1).

Throughout the story, the reader is reminded of the real world in which Benjamin Button lives. This allows him to mimic and thus question the reactions of the people of Baltimore, and ultimately America, to someone who does not conform to the social norm. Benjamin's life spans three wars in which the United States were involved: the Civil War in his early years, the Spanish-American War, in which he participated, and World War I. For the latter, he wanted to return to the military in order to support the Allied war efforts. He even went to Camp Mosby, another real place serving as setting for the special story of Benjamin Button, where he got declined because he was deemed too young.

As we can see, Fitzgerald consciously set the fictional story in reality to question the expectations the American society in the 19th and early 20th century had from a person of a certain age (Port 13). "This narrative technique […] forces the reader to take the protagonist as a symbolic and an 'as-if- real' character at the same time", as Basseler (3) points out. The reader, of course, recognizes that Benjamin's absurd story is not real and can never become real, but what it symbolizes - the pursuit of "unpredictable or queer temporal trajectories in relation to time's arrow" (Medovoi 658) - brings out the society's strange norms regarding the course of life.

Changes in the Protagonist's Relationships

In the short story, Benjamin Button's relationships with three people are examined in particular detail: his father Roger, his wife Hildegard, and his son Roscoe. These represent different times in the protagonist's life.

In the early years of his life, Benjamin's relationship with his father is prominent. At his birth, Roger Button is shocked at first. He is ashamed of the baby's visual appearance and immediately worries about society's reactions: "People would stop to speak to him, and what was he going to say? He would have to introduce this—this septuagenarian" (Fitzgerald 6). Here we see how hard a man like Roger Button tries to conform to social norms. To do so, he even goes so far as to buy Benjamin baby food and toys in order to deceive society (Fitzgerald 10). Based on his 5 foot 8 height alone, Benjamin would never be perceived as a baby or even a toddler. Nevertheless, his father tries to rejuvenate his appearance by dying his hair, which illustrates society's aversion to old age.

When Benjamin meets his future wife Hildegard, they are both twenty years old. Since Hildegard prefers a 50-year-old man and Benjamin is exactly that physical age, he conceals his normal age (Fitzgerald 16). When they made their engagement public, rumors swirled about Benjamin's age and identity. Society and even his father Roger did not approve of the perceived age disparity. Here, it becomes clear that "age serves as a crucial axis of social and semiotic difference in its own right, with tremendous implications [for] life courses" (Medovoi 657). Fitzgerald's criticism of the rigid social rules of the time is particularly evident in the fact that Benjamin and Hildegard paid no attention even to the visual age difference, which makes Benjamin the happiest he has been and will be in the following years (Basseler 4).

However, this happiness continues to swing into dissatisfaction, because while Benjamin is getting younger and younger, Hildegard is aging. Interestingly, this feeling is already apparent when they are both 35. This is the only time Benjamin's chronological and physical age coincide, and while he is very successful professionally and socially, his marriage no longer satisfies him (Fitzgerald 19). This displays the different life courses of men and women at the time. As Port puts it, "Benjamin's 'curious case' of un-aging is set against the normative chronology of his beloved [wife], for whom the emotional challenges and perceived loss of social value associated with aging for women are intensified by her lover's reversed trajectory" (14). Women were still seen mainly as mothers and housewives. A woman's life path was to be raised to be a housewife, find a high-status man, and bear him children. A professional career and the self-fulfillment that comes with it is hardly possible for her, and so her value to society is seen as declining even at a comparatively young age. This perspective of society is embodied here by Hildegard as "female aging implies loss of attractiveness and femininity" (Wohlmann 51). Furthermore, it shows that Benjamin Button is not only a victim of social norms, but also applies them himself to his fellow human beings.

The relationship with his son Roscoe is initially rather positive. The two are often mistaken for brothers and eventually Benjamin leaves the family business to his son (Fitzgerald 23). However, this changes as the age difference between them increases: "[T]here was […] a tendency on his son's part to think that Benjamin [...] was somewhat in the way" (Fitzgerald 23). This tendency grew stronger as Roscoe had to care more and more for the now infant Benjamin. This is also evidenced by his opinion "that his father, in refusing to look sixty, had not behaved like a 'red-blooded he-man'".

This dislike of Benjamin is very reminiscent of the way his father perceived him in his early years. Both as an old man and as an infant, Benjamin is disrespected and considered to be in the way. Only in his adult years is he successful and socially respected, since his chronological, physical and psychological age coincide and he is at the peak of his powers there. Wohlmann formulates this progression of life from a social perspective as follows: "Until adulthood, early developments tend to be told as progress narratives, whereas later changes in life are imagined as decline narratives" (43). Even though Benjamin's life proceeds in the exact opposite direction, this is also true for him and again highlights Fitzgerald's critique of societal values in relation to the aging process.

Challenging the Concept of Age

The central point Fitzgerald's wants to make with his short story *The Curious Case of Benjamin Button* is to challenge the modern life-course model and our concept of aging in general. Benjamin Button is rarely respected because he does not look or behave according to his age. Thus, we can see that one has to follow a certain life course in order to "have the possibility to become a valuable member of society" (Basseler 6).

It is noteworthy, however, that Benjamin Button still manages to live a quite successful life, if we neglect the chronological order of his achievements: he goes to college, runs a successful business, becomes a war veteran, gets married and has a son. As Basseler points out: "[H]is life is not a succession of random events, but follows a highly conventionalized and pre-structured pattern, the 'normal biography'" (7). Hence, Benjamin's life contains all the successes which the modern society would expect of an American man with his social status. If these achievements do not come at the right age, it can have corresponding effects:

> Success, career, and wealth as the hallmarks of economic thinking appear as directly connected to age and self-esteem. If success or wealth are not available at a particular age in a man's life, an aging crisis can occur (Wohlmann 51).

Still, there are only few points in his life where he is treated with respect - in fact, only his adult years between 25 and 50 in which his chronological and physical age are rather close to each other. With the help of Benjamin Button's successes and the simultaneous low esteem by his fellow human beings, Fitzgerald "exposes the social administration of human lifetime" and criticizes the conventionalized life-course model (Basseler 6).

In fact, this criticism can be applied to a much larger picture. It's not just the order in which we should achieve certain achievements in our lives that Fitzgerald challenges, but the now conventionalized goals that every valued member of society must have. Marriage and reproduction at the family level, as well as a high level of education and a professional career, were then as now part of the expectations of men (Freeman 4). If someone does not want to give in to these expectations, he will not be a part of society.

There are two groups in society whose role in society Fitzgerald continues to question: women and the elderly. Through Hildegard he shows the role of women as housewives and mothers. Once she has reached her 30's, she is not seen as attractive anymore. Fitzgerald calls for women to be seen differently and more individual freedom in their lives by his depiction of Hildegard. Besides that, Benjamin Button's adult years may be successful, but his early years are characterized by the problem of fitting in. He is seen as a burden, as he isn't able to work because of his physical age of 70. Here, Fitzgerald tries to change the narrative regarding old age, neglecting the perceptions of decline and decay.

Conclusion and Final Remarks

Over the course of this paper, it was shown that time has always played its part in narratives. However, plots usually followed a linear and chronological course. In the Modern Period, however, time moved into the foreground, promoted by the industrialization. As a result, Fitzgerald and others writers of the Jazz Age wrote stories in which time kind of became a character itself. One of these narratives is the short story *The Curious Case of Benjamin Button*, which deals with the process of aging and the life-course model of the time. Back then, men like the protagonist were expected to achieve certain things on a professional and private level at a particular age. Furthermore, old age was closely associated with mortality.

We have seen that Fitzgerald achieves to challenge these prevailing age roles by reversing Benjamin Button's life. In fact, only his physical age moves in the other direction, whereas his chronological age runs in the same direction as his environment. By situating the story in the US state Baltimore from the Civil War to WW1, he creates a closer connection to the society he challenges. He displays what he considers society's erroneous expectations regarding age roles through Benjamin's relationships with his father, wife and son. In addition to the strict life-course model, he also questions the role of women at the time and demands another perspective on old age.

The Curious Case of Benjamin Button has not been a success right after it has been published. Nowadays, it is considered one of the greatest short stories ever. Indeed, Fitzgerald's criticism is in some aspects still valid today. We still mostly follow the same life-course model which has been considered the norm back then and those who deviate from it are still seen as outsiders at least by some people. The process of aging is still associated with decline and it is counteracted with rejuvenation projects such as plastic surgery.

Nevertheless, there is greater individual freedom in what we do in our lives and in what order. Changing careers or still going to university as an adult is nothing special anymore. Furthermore, having children is not seen as necessary for a woman's life to be considered successful. In general, women enjoy a much greater freedom in what they want to do with their lives and are not seen as housewives anymore. The fact that deviations from the supposed norm like not having children are not viewed as negative has changed since the Jazz Age and is of enormous importance, for example, with regard to the LGBTQ+ community. In this respect, our society has developed more towards individuality and less conformity.

References

Basseler, Michael. "A Normal Biography Reversed: The Temporalization of Life in F. Scott Fitzgerald's 'The Curious Case of Benjamin Button.'" *Journal of the Short Story in English*, vol. 64, 2015.

Fitzgerald, Francis S. *The Curious Case of Benjamin Button*. Feedbooks, 1922.

Freeman, Elizabeth. *Time Binds: Queer Temporalities, Queer Histories*. Duke University Press, 2010.

Gullette, Margaret M. *Aged by Culture*. University of Chicago Press, 2004.

Medovoi, Leerom. "Age Trouble: A Timely Subject in American Literary and Cultural Studies." *American Literary History*, vol. 22, 2010.

Miller, Hillis J. "Time in Literature." *Daedalus*, vol. 132, 2003.

Port, Cynthia. "No Future? Aging, Temporality, History, and Reverse Chronologies." *Occasion: Interdisciplinary Studies in the Humanities*, vol. 4, 2011.

Ricoeur, Paul. "Narrative Time." *Critical Inquiry*, vol. 7, 1980.

Time in Literature – Exactly What Is Time? www.exactlywhatistime.com/other-aspects-of-time/time-in-literature. Accessed 11 Oct. 2022.

Wohlmann, Anita. *Aged Young Adults: Age Readings of Contemporary American Novels and Films*. Transcript, 2014.

YOUR KNOWLEDGE HAS VALUE

- We will publish your bachelor's and master's thesis, essays and papers

- Your own eBook and book - sold worldwide in all relevant shops

- Earn money with each sale

Upload your text at www.GRIN.com and publish for free